Mom
A Friendship Discovered

by Emily Williams-Wheeler

Adventure Publications, Inc.
Cambridge, Minnesota

Copyright ©1996 by Emily Williams-Wheeler
Published by
Adventure Publications, Inc.
P.O. Box 269
Cambridge, MN 55008
All rights reserved
Printed in Hong Kong
ISBN 1-885061-67-6

As time goes by

I see how much we have in common.

But I wonder, how can I ever
be the person you are?

You've always been there
to lighten my troubles

and to handle life's turns.

Impending deadlines
have sparked creativity

and brought us to work as a team.

Together, we have cooked up
as many meals as memories.

Your healing kisses
and words of wisdom

have diminished the pain
of scrapes and scares —

While your confidence has pushed
me to succeed on my own.

You have stood by me at my worst

and applauded me at my best.

With summer came the
sunbonnets and sunscreen,

Ice-cold lemonade and
Snickerdoodle cookies.

You prepared soothing baths
to remove sand and salt.

and turned back fresh sheets
for a comfortable sleep.

I dared to venture out
into the cold world,

knowing hot chocolate and warm, dry clothes awaited.

Yesterday your rooms were
decorated by the heart,

today photographs replace
the childish drawings

Your generous hugs have
carried me from toddler to adult

and though I am
no longer a little girl,
you'll always be my mother

and, even more, my friend.

I love you, Mom.

For more information
on books by
Emily Williams-Wheeler,
contact your local
gift / book store or
Adventure Publications
1·800·678·7006.